BONUS

Want a Bonus?

Download The Vision Board Freebie:
5 Steps to Create a Vision Board that Works E-Book
&
Vision Board Goal Setting Workbook
Link: bit.ly/vision_board_freebie

60 Positive Affirmation cards + 30 Inspirational quote cards For Vision Boards

I AM CAPABLE AND I AM STRONG.

YOU LEARN MORE FROM FAILURE THAN SUCCESS. DON'T LET IT STOP YOU. FAILURE BUILDS CHARACTER

IF I WANT SOMETHING BADLY ENOUGH, I CAN FIND A WAY TO MAKE IT HAPPEN.

I AM BRAVE, RESILIENT AND STRONG.

THE FUTURE MAY BE UNCERTAIN BUT THAT WON'T STOP ME LOOKING FORWARD WITH HOPE.

ONLY SURROUND YOURSELF WITH PEOPLE WHO WILL LIFT YOU HIGHER

60 Positive Affirmation cards + 30 Inspirational quote cards For Your Vision Board

DOWNLOAD

Link: bit.ly/affirmations-quotes-cards

Or Use QR Code

FOLLOW US

Instagram QR Code

MANIFESTHAPPINESSCHANNEL

Follow Us On Instagram: @manifesthappinesschannel
Subscribe to Our Youtube Channel:
youtube.com/c/manifesthappinesschannel

MANIFEST HAPPINESS

For More Vision Board Clip Art Books
Visit Our Page on AMAZON

Link: bit.ly/mh_press

or Use QR Code

We Have Vision Board Clip Art Books For :

Women, Men, Teens, Kids, Travel, Self-love, Weight Loss, Wedding, Word Art, Health, Affirmations, Vision Board Parties, Business & Money and more

Money

Winner

Success

Online Business

Business Owner

Employed

LOVE

Got Married

Proposal

big happy family

Family

Friends

Drink Water

healthy food
physical exercise
no smoking
not drink

Good Sleep

GYM
Fitness

Travel the World

Yoga

Meditation

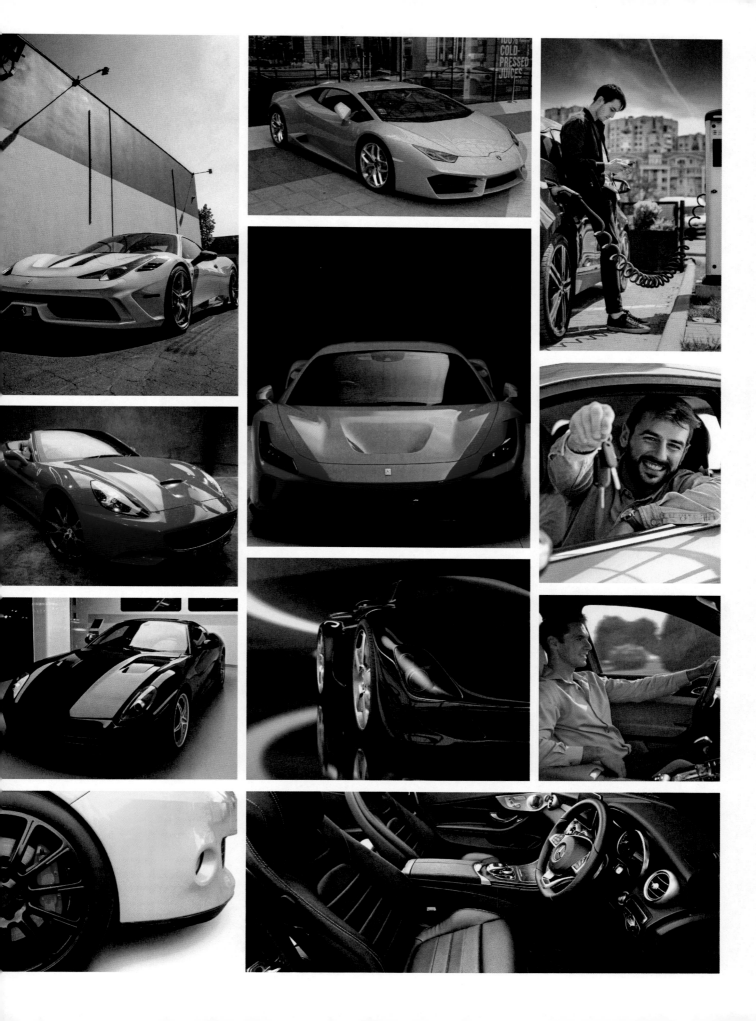

home
sweet home

home

Luxury

It always SEEMS IMPOSSIBLE until it's DONE

Don't WAIT FOR opportunity, CREATE it

SMALL changes CAN MAKE huge DIFFERENCE

STEP OUT OF YOUR comfort ZONE

IF YOU CAN Dream IT YOU CAN DO IT

All THINGS are POSSIBLE IF YOU Believe

EVERY journey NEEDS A first STEP

Live WITHOUT REGRETS

Believe in yourself AND YOU'LL BE unstoppable

Made in the USA
Las Vegas, NV
27 December 2024

15431323R00024